SO-AHA-848

Irish Jokes

Irish Jokes

Compiled by Donovan Pilley

LAGAN BOOKS

This edition published 2001 by Geddes & Grosset, an imprint of
Children's Leisure Products Limited

Compiled by Donovan Pilley

© 2001 Children's Leisure Products Limited, David Dale House,
New Lanark, ML11 9DJ, Scotland

Illustrations by Mark Mechan

All rights reserved. No part of this publication may be
reproduced, stored in a retrieval system, or transmitted,
in any form or by any means, electronic, mechanical,
photocopying, recording or otherwise, without
the prior permission of the copyright holder

ISBN 1 84205 071 0

Printed and bound in Europe

A poor family had no rights to the turf bog, and, at the time the neighbours were digging their peat, the son of the house sat at the door, watching the carts go by with their loads. Then, seeing one sod fall from a cart, he had an idea. Spiking the sod of turf on a stick, he set it up in the ground. As each cart went by, he shouted,

"Hey, lads, can you hit the mark?"

None of them could resist hurling a peat at the stick, and by the end of the day, the lad had amassed a tidy pile without leaving his cottage door.

A soldier in an Irish regiment in the American Civil War was wounded in battle, and lay on the field groaning and crying out. At last his cries so irritated another member of his company, in a similar plight, that he called out, "Damn you, stop making that noise. D'you think nobody is killed but yourself?"

The farmer O'Dowd had been invited to supper by his neighbour, Cassidy. Knowing it would be a long and late evening he took his big stable lantern with him. After a convivial session, he set off for home, and reached it safely, clutching his lantern firmly all the way.

Early next morning, there was a rap on

the door. He stumbled down to open it, and there was his neighbour, Cassidy.

"Here's your lamp, O'Dowd," he said, "and would you mind letting me have my parrot and cage back."

A farmer returning from a trip to the market remarked:

"Well, I didn't get as much for my bull as I expected; but then, I didn't expect I would."

A Scotsman, an Englishman and an Irishman were caught shoplifting in Paris in the year 1789, and were condemned to the guillotine. The Scotsman lay down on the scaffold with his head on the block, the executioner pulled the handle, and nothing happened. The blade was stuck. The Scotsman was let off, and staggered away in relief. When the Englishman lay down, exactly the same thing happened. Then it was the Irishman's turn. But before putting his head on the block, he tapped the executioner on the shoulder.

"I can see what's wrong," he said. "If you'd only tweak out that bit of twig blocking the pulley, she'll come down as sweet as you like."

An Irish labouring bricklayer laid a wager with his companion and fellow-labourer that he could not carry him on his hod up a ladder to the top of a high house and bring him down again safely; the bet was taken and won. As Pat, who rode upon the hod, alighted, he said: "By Jasus, he tripped once as we were coming down, and I was in hopes I should have won my wager."

A small boy, when asked how old he and his brother were, replied, "He's ten and I'm eight, but in two years time I'll have caught him up."

"**W**ill you hurry up!" called Mr Corcoran to his wife. "If you don't get a move on we'll be late."

"Will you stop your nagging," she shouted. "I've been telling you for the past hour – I'll be ready in a minute."

A countryman, being interviewed for a job by a strong farmer, was asked if he could live hard.

"By faith, your Honour," he replied, "so long as your Honour feeds me well, I could live on nothing but bread and water."

A blind man was out for a walk with a friend, and as they crossed a field, the friend suddenly realised that there was a bull in it. A moment later the bull saw them, and charged at them from behind. The friend, terrified, took to his heels, leaving the blind man walking on. The bull was so surprised to see someone calmly walking on, paying no attention, not even turning round, that his furious gallop slowed to a walk, and he came up behind and with his snout just nudged the blind man in the back. Immediately the man turned, stretched out his arms, seized the horns, and with a twist flipped the astonished bull onto its side, where it lay in shock. The friend returned to the scene.

"Man, that was brave," he said. "I never saw anything like it."

"He's lucky," replied the blind man. "I just got the handlebars of his bicycle. If I'd got a grip of himself, I'd have given him the devil of a hiding."

For Irish Stew: take 1 pound of stewing lamb, two large onions, four pounds of potatoes, six pints of stout. Open and consume the stout. Forget the rest.

In some parts of Ireland the sleep that knows no waking is followed by the wake that knows no sleeping.

What's the difference between a Kerry wedding and a Kerry wake?
  There's one drunk less at the wake.

An Irish visitor sat listening as an English politician ranted on in a long speech.

"I was born an Englishman, and I have lived as an Englishman, and I hope to die an Englishman!" cried the speaker.

The Irishman turned to his neighbour. "Has the man no ambition at all?" he whispered.

Alternative Lines from Irish Literature:

**Believe me, if all these endearing
  young charms,
Which I gaze on so fondly today,
Were to change by tomorrow and fleet
  in my arms,
I would run like the blazes away.**

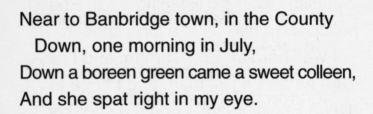

Near to Banbridge town, in the County
   Down, one morning in July,
Down a boreen green came a sweet colleen,
And she spat right in my eye.

**There's a dear little plant that grows in
  our isle
And if you smoke it you'll end up in jyle.**

The harp that once through Tara's halls
The soul of music shed,
Now hangs quite mute on Tara's walls –
They've karaoke instead.

~~~~~~~~~~

**Down by the Salley Gardens my love
  and I did meet;
She'd stepped on something squishy
  with her little snow-white feet.**

~~~~~~~~~~

I once loved a boy, just a bold Irish boy,
Who'd come and who'd go at my request;
But mostly I would ask him to go,
Because of his smelly vest.

~~~~~~~~~~

**Mellow, the moonlight its shine is
  beginning;
Close by the window young Eileen is
  sinning.**

~~~~~~~~~~

~~~~~~~~~~~~~~~

Kathleen Mavourneen! The grey dawn is
　　breaking,
The horn of the hunter is heard on the hill;
Wake up, my girl, it's time you were taking
Your regular morning-after pill.

~~~~~~~~~~~~~~~

**In Dublin's fair city, where girls are so
　　pretty,
A striking exception
　　was Molly Malone.**

~~~~~~~~~~~~~~~

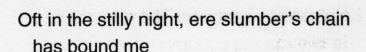

Oft in the stilly night, ere slumber's chain
  has bound me
I find the eiderdown has slipped off from
  around me.

~~~~~~~~~~

**Oh, Danny boy, the pipes, the pipes
  are calling,
From glen to glen, and down the
  mountainside,
The noise they make is truly quite
  appalling,
'Twould make a music-lover run and
  hide.**

A Dubliner sent a message to a farmer he knew in the country:

"Please send bag of potatoes. If good, will send cheque."

He got a message back.

"Please send cheque. If good, will send potatoes."

Two men were passing some blackberry bushes, while the fruits were still unripe.

"It's ridiculous to call them blackberries, when they are red," said one.

His friend said: "Don't you know that blackberries are always red when they are green?"

Farmer Gilligan: "My bull fell down in a hole. I had to shoot him."

Farmer Gilhaney: "You shot him in the hole?"

Farmer Gilligan: "No, I shot him in the head."

A member of the landed gentry was stopped for speeding on the motorway to Dublin Airport.

"Do you know who I am?" the man protested. "I am a member of one of Ireland's oldest families."

"So what?" said the cop. "We're not after ya for breeding from."

Some of the Achievements of Dermot O'Boyligan, the Clonakility Inventor:

An ejector seat for helicopter pilots.

A crop spray that kills the crops so that the insects starve to death.

Perforated Wellington boots that let water drain out of them.

The O'Boyligan belt-mounted cantilever for armless violin players.

The eesi-empty coal bag, open at each end.

The disposable soup plate that dissolves in water.

Transparent fabric suits for nudists to wear on cold days.

A passer-by on the outskirts of a small country village saw a young girl struggling to drive a reluctant cow along the road.

"Can you manage all right?" he asked.

"I'm just taking it along to the bull," she explained, as the cow jerked its head and mooed angrily.

"Couldn't your father do that?" asked the man.

"Oh, no," said the child. "It has to be the bull."

The worst thing about him is, when he's not drunk, he's sober.

"**B**y Jasus," said a farmer in earlier times, "the clergy are the very devil for collecting tithes. Be a farmer ever so poor, they'll take their tenth; heaven help us, I would not be surprised if some of them tried to take a twentieth."

"**H**ow old was the deceased?" asked an observer at a funeral.

"Oh, very old," replied one of the mourners. "He was eighty-five."

"That's not so old," returned the other. "Why, if my own father was alive today, he'd be a hundred and twelve."

Sentenced by the warship's captain to a dozen lashes, a seaman fled up into the rigging of the vessel and clung to the mast-head, where no-one could reach him.

"Come down, you rascal," roared the captain. "Come down this instant or I'll give you two dozen."

"I won't," called the man. "I won't come down, no, not if you was to make it four dozen."

When a lady observed one day how bright and beautiful the sunshine was, a friend of hers replied:

"That's all very well, but the moon is much more useful. It gives us light at night, when we really need it; the sun just shines all day when it's broad daylight anyway."

A citizen of Mallow, sitting at a Dublin supper table, heard the Sphinx mentioned, and whispered to his neighbour:

"The Sphinx, who is that now?"

"A monster, man," replied the neighbour.

"You don't say so? And I thought I knew everybody who was anybody in Munster!"

A country gentleman ordered a new pair of leather boots from the cobbler. As the measurements were taken, they observed one of his legs was bigger than the other, and it was agreed that the cobbler would make the boots accordingly. When they arrived, the purchaser put the big boot on the small leg and struggled in vain to get the big leg into the small boot. Taking them back in a rage, he exclaimed,

"Oh, you thief of the world, I ordered one boot bigger than the other and instead you have made one boot smaller than the other."

A young man had just announced to his uncle that he planned to study for the priesthood. The uncle was overjoyed.

"I couldn't be more pleased," he said. "I hope to live to hear you preach at my funeral."

May you never live to see your wife a widow.
May you be in Heaven for half an hour before the Devil knows you're dead.
May your friends have fine weather for your funeral.

Better to be a coward for a moment than a dead hero for the rest of your life.

An Irishman, it's said, will die before he lets himself be buried outside Ireland.

"**H**ave you seen Rafferty lately?"

"Well, yes and no."

"How do you mean, yes and no?"

"Well, I saw someone I thought was him, and he saw someone he thought was me, but when we got up to each other we saw it wasn't either of us."

"When I first saw you, I thought it was you, but now I see it is your brother."

The auctioneer declared: "Every item on sale here will be sold to the highest bidder, unless someone else offers more."

"Madam," said the serving girl, "there's a poor man at the door with a wooden leg."

"Well, tell him I don't need any wooden legs today."

"I saw a really beautiful dress in that boutique," said Maureen. "It would have fitted me perfectly, if I could have got into it."

"Your Honour, we find the man who stole the mare Not Guilty."

"What became of old Dan McGrew?"

"Didn't you hear? He was sentenced to be hanged but he saved his life by dying in prison."

What is an alibi?

An alibi is the ability to be in two places at once.

When Mr McTurk's wife died suddenly, the Gardai came along, to ask him a few questions.

"What were her last words to you?" asked an officer.

"Phew, that's a hard question to answer," he replied.

"Why so?"

"She spoke without interruption for forty-four years."

When a friend of Captain O'Neill fell ill, the captain warned him:

"Do not send for Dr Slane."

"Why not?" asked the invalid.

"Well, when I was ill, he came to see me, and filled me that full of potions and powders, that I stayed ill for a good two weeks after I was well again."

Terence Molloy was a great enthusiast for the drink. Every evening he would go down to the pub and he would come back drunk. This was very vexing to his wife. She was at her wits' end for what to do. Then she had an idea. Terence always took a short-cut home, on a path that led through the churchyard.

She decided that she give him a scare
that would get him off the drink forever.

She got hold of a pair of goat horns, a
devil-mask and an old red curtain, and
made them into a costume for herself.
Then, late one moonlit evening, she
disguised herself in this and hid behind
a tall tombstone. In due course Terence
came along, stumbling slightly and
singing in a slurred voice. His wife

stepped out from behind her hiding-place, ready to give him a terrible warning. But Terence rocked back on his heels and eyed the apparition.

"I am the Devil!" she roared.

"Pleased to meet you," said Terence. "We're sort of related. I'm married to your sister."

"Martin, can you spell 'paint'?" asked the teacher.

"Which colour, miss?" he asked.

Ireland's Champion Squash Player: Rick O'Shea

When a lady was buying a dress length, she asked the merchant if it was durable stuff.

"It will wear for ever, madam, and make you a petticoat afterwards," he replied.

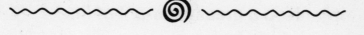

At the end of a sociable evening, a guest was looking for his coat.

Sure, you're wearing it," said his host.

"Why, so I am," he said, looking down. "I'm so glad you told me, or I'd have gone home without it."

I would have been a man of considerable property, if only my father had never entered the family.

A country gentleman had just organised a great clear-out of his house and stables, and was wondering with his steward what to do with the great pile of rubbish that had resulted.

"I will get a great pit dug, and have it all put in there," said the steward.

"Yes, but what about the earth from the pit?" inquired his master.

"Oh, I'll get the pit made deep enough to hold that too."

It was perhaps the same steward who, having cut a hole in the back door, big enough for the cat to come in through, went on to cut a smaller one, for her kittens.

A man was in court for non-payment of maintenance to his estranged wife. After hearing the case, the judge said:

"I have decided to give her an extra ten pounds a week."

"Bless your Honour," said the man. "You're very kind to do that. Maybe I'll send her a few shillings myself, as well."

One fine day, two old men were sitting on a seat in the market square.

"It's fine weather that's in it," one remarked.

"Indeed," said the other. "Such grand weather, I'm sorry I'm not still working, so that I could take the day off."

An Irish gentleman, showing off his cabinet of pictures to a group of friends, was made anxious by the way they all crowded in:

"Faith, gentlemen, if you all go in there together, it won't hold you."

"I hear Old Boylan died last week."
"Aye, 'tis true."
"Was he ill then?"
"No, he died in the best of health."

A beautiful Irish lady was presented at court to King George III, who politely hoped that since her arrival in London, she had been able to see all the sights and entertainments.

"Oh, yes, please your Majesty," she replied. "I believe I've seen every sight in London worth seeing, except a coronation."

"Oh, Maureen, why won't you marry me?" demanded Kevin, then, suddenly suspicious: "There isn't anyone else, is there?"

"Oh, Kevin," sighed Maureen. "If only there could be."

"Tell me this," said Mr Kelly to Mr Keogh, "what is it that we have wives for?"

After some thought, Mr Keogh said: "Well, it's for the things that go wrong that you can't blame the government for."

He: If I was to propose to you,
  Kathleen, would you say 'Yes'?"
She: "If you thought I would say 'Yes',
  Danny, would you propose to me?"

"How's your wife?"
"She's very sick."
"Oh, dangerous?"
"No, she's too weak to
  be dangerous."

One man is as good as another, and often a damn sight better.

A Tralee man came to Dublin for a few days and decided to get his hair cut at a smart hairdresser's. He went into the salon and asked:

"How much is a haircut?"

"Haircuts start at fifteen pounds."

Wow, he thought, I didn't expect it to be that much.

"What about a shave?" he asked.

"That would be five pounds."

He sat down in the chair.

"Shave my head, then," he said.

Surveying her new class, the teacher said:
"All I want out of you is silence, and not too much of that, either."

Doolan was looking particularly miserable.

"My wife told me today that she believes in free love," he said to his friend Devane.

"Well, that's all right, mine does too," said Devane.

"But you always seem to be such a devoted couple," said Doolan.

"And so we are," said Devane. "She wouldn't dream of charging me."

A wife had brought money to the marriage and never allowed her husband to forget it. When a visitor remarked on the piano, she said:

"If it wasn't for my money, we wouldn't have it."

When the visitor admired a picture on the wall, she said:

"Yes, it was my money bought us that."

When the visitor complimented them on the new silk curtains, she said:

"If it wasn't for my money, they wouldn't be here."

"If it wasn't for your money," muttered her husband, not quite quietly enough, "I wouldn't be here either."

Mrs Milligan went to see a solicitor in her home town.

"I want to divorce my husband."

"I see," said the solicitor. "Do you have a grudge?"

"No," said Mrs Milligan, "We keep the car on the pavement."

"Does your husband beat you up?"

"No," she replied, "it's me that's always up first making him a cup o' tea."

The solicitor sighed.

"Does he go in for any, ah, funny business. You know, in bed."

"The man couldn't crack a joke to save his life," said Mrs Milligan.

"Well, what are your grounds?" asked the solicitor.

"Grounds? We have no grounds. We live on the third floor."

"Mrs Milligan," said the solicitor, "I'm trying to establish why you want to divorce your husband."

"It's because he's an impossible man to hold an intelligent conversation with."

As the groom stood beside his bride-to-be, the priest observed that his eyes were crossing and un-crossing, that he could scarcely stand upright, and that a powerful odour of drink was coming from him.

"I can't possibly marry you in this state," he said severely. "He'll have to come back when he's sober."

"Oh, please Father, carry on." she cried. "He won't come back, if he's sober."

Arriving at Knock Airport, an American visitor saw a stall with "Unusual Irish Souvenirs" over it and went across to have a look. The first thing that caught his eye was a human skull, labelled "St Patrick's Skull – a unique opportunity to acquire this remarkable relic. Guaranteed Genuine."

"How much?" asked the visitor, and though he was disconcerted to find out the price, he paid up and went off with the skull carefully wrapped in a copy of *The Knock Weekly Knocker*. He took the skull home, and treasured it for many years. Much later in life, he revisited Ireland and went again to Knock. Seeing the "Unusual Souvenirs" stall still there, he went to look, and was

more than surprised to see "St Patrick's Skull" again on sale.

"But I bought that from you twenty years ago!" he protested to the stall-holder. The man scratched his head.

"The thing was," he said. "What you bought was St Patrick's skull, all right. But yours was when he was grown up. This one here is from St Patrick when he was just a boy."

The parish atheist died, and the priest came to pay his condolences to the household. As he left, he commented to himself.

"Sad, really. There he was, all dressed up, and nowhere to go."

Great Short Books of Our Time:

Arm Movements for Irish Dance

Ireland: Centre of World Cricket

Hurling for Softies

The Kerryman as Romantic Lover

Banana-Growing in Your Irish Garden

Collected Christmas Goodwill Messages from the Moderator of the Free Presbyterian Church to His Holiness the Pope

The Irishman's Guide to Helping About the House

The Guide to Irish Motorway Service Stations

Things to Do on a Dry Day in Donegal

In Praise of Country Bungalows

On his first visit to New York, a Connemara man was astonished by the speed and volume of the traffic. Wanting to cross Fifth Avenue, he went to an intersection where a traffic cop was controlling the flow.

"Pedestrians now!" called the cop, holding his arm up to stop the cars. The man waited. The cop waved the traffic on. After a while he held up his arm again:

"Pedestrians cross!" he shouted. People pushed past the man, but he stayed in place. Again the cop waved the cars on. The man looked cross.

"Fair do's," he shouted to the policeman. "That's twice in a row you've let the pedestrians through. What about the Catholics?"

Children are the curse of this country – especially if you don't have any.

Everything here is perfectly abnormal. (A Dublin saying.)

What's the world to a man, If his wife is a widdy?

The most popular speaker is the one who sits down before he gets up.

A man sitting in a restaurant said to his companion: "I'm nearly sure that the man over there in the corner is my old school friend Haggerty."

"Why don't you go over and say hello," said his companion.

"I don't think I will," said the man. "You see, the thing is, he's so shy he would feel awkward if it turned out he was the wrong man."

God bless the Holy Trinity.

(A motto seen on a banner in a Dublin religious procession.)

Looking round the greybeards in the village pub, the visitor asked:

"How old is the oldest man in the place?"

"Oh, we don't have an oldest man any more," said one of the locals. "He died last week."

A particularly lean citizen, encountering a similarly-shaped friend, said:

"I have just been speaking to our old friend, Terence O'Hare. He is grown so thin, I scarcely knew him; you may be thin, and I may be thin but, by faith, he's thinner than both of us put together!"

Sentencing to death a man who had been found guilty of stealing a clock, a judge remarked to the criminal: "By grasping at time, you have enabled yourself to attain eternity."

A clergyman was reading the burial service in the course of a funeral. Coming to the lines which refer to "our dear brother, or sister," he realised that he had forgotten the sex of the departed, and whispered to a man standing close by: "Is it a brother or a sister?"

"Ah, neither," said the man, "just a cousin."

A passenger riding into Dublin on an outside car, noticing the wretched appearance of the horse as it staggered along, said to the driver:

"Really, it's cruelty to such an animal to drive it along like this."

"Your honour," replied the driver, "it would be cruelty to a wife and seven children if I did not."

There was an illiterate man who tried to sue the baker for forging his signature on hot cross buns.

Two gentlemen were walking down Grafton Street in Dublin, just as the maids were out mopping the doorsteps. One of them placed her bucket in such a way that one of the men inadvertently kicked it.

"Oh, my dear man," said his friend. "I am sorry to see you have kicked the bucket at last."

"Not at all," said the man. "I have only turned a little pail."

Danny was walking by the pub when he saw a bright and shiny new motorbike parked outside it, with the key still in the lock. Thinking he would like to try a ride, he wheeled it quietly away to a place

where the sound of the engine would not be heard, started it up, and away he went. He was having a fine spin, but soon he felt cold. So he stopped and put his jacket on back to front, and turned his cap round with its peak to the back, to keep the wind off him. Then he set off again. Going faster now, he lost control of the machine, hit the bank of the road, and went flying off, just where some people were at work in a field. The accident was duly reported to the Gardai, and an officer came to the scene.

"Was it instant death, then?" he asked the witnesses.

"No, he was alive lying in the road," said one. "But as soon as we set his head straight, he died."

Two men were walking from Mallow to Cork. Towards the end of the day they were getting very weary and footsore, and one of them expressed a wish to sleep the night in a barn, and go on the next day. Just then they encountered a countryman and asked him how far it was to Cork.

"Ten miles," he said.

"Ten miles!" cried the other man, turning to his friend. "Man, between the two of us, that's only five miles each. We'll walk on and be there easy as anything."

A Dublin girl found herself pregnant. The father was a penniless Dutch sailor. She confided her trouble to her best friend.

"But didn't you also go to bed with young Cadogan, son of the rich farmer at Clane? Why not place the blame on him?"

"I was thinking that myself," said the mother-to-be. "But what will come of it when the baby starts to speak, and it is spouting the Dutch language?"

Mr Kogan, hammering at the door: "Is it dead or alive you are in there?"

Mr Grogan, from within: "It's neither I am, but sleepin'."

"How can you tell your twin boys apart, Mrs Sullivan?" asked a neighbour.

"Oh, it's not difficult. If I put my finger in wee Sean's mouth and he bites me, I know it's wee Pat."

Mrs Grundie had been to the dressmaker's to be measured for a new skirt.

"What did she say about that big bum of yours?" asked Mr Grundie.

"Your name was never mentioned," she said coldly.

At the Limerick fair a countryman bought a mare from a horse-dealer. The dealer promised him that the animal was sound in wind and limb, and faultless in all respects. After buying the horse, the purchaser discovered that it was blind in one eye, and almost so in the other. Returning to find the dealer, he complained bitterly about being tricked by lies.

"Not a word of a lie is there in it," said the dealer, refusing to repay the price. "The poor creature is almost blind, that is true. But that is not her fault: it is her misfortune."

Two unemployed men were strolling along a country lane when they came to a sign that said: "Tree Fellers Wanted".

"D'you see that, Seamus?" said Mike. "If only my brother Vinnie was here too, we'd all get a job."

Teacher: What is the male of a cow?
Boy: Grass.

"Is it very noisy where you live?"

"I'll say it is. It's so noisy we only ever get any peace when a plane coming into the airport drowns out the noise of the traffic on the motorway."

"If you don't leave me alone," shouted Doreen to Dermot, "I'll go and find someone who will!"

A couple were writing begging letters when they heard their lottery numbers read out on the television.

"We've won a million pounds Dermot!" shrieked his wife.

"Okay, okay," said Dermot. "Just finish off the letters."

Three priests from the West were travelling by train to a meeting in Dublin. To while away the time, one said:

"We've known each other a long time, but we don't really know each other very well. Why don't we each tell one thing about ourselves that we keep a dark and deadly secret? Even men of the cloth can have a human weakness. We'll feel better for confiding it, and we'll know one another all the better."

Seeing the other two look rather reluctant, he went on:

"I'll start. All my parishioners think I'm a most abstemious man, but every now and then I go on the bottle and get drunk for days at a time. They all think I'm on holiday."

This prompted the next one to say:

"My own weakness is gambling. Every now and then I can't resist putting money on the horses. I'm afraid that's where the money for the choir outing went."

They turned to the third priest.

"And what about you?"

"Me?" he said, with a serene smile. "My only weakness is that sometimes I just can't help gossiping and giving away things people tell me in confidence."

Some time after his resignation, an Anglican Archbishop of Dublin paid a visit to his successor. Back in the archiepiscopal palace, at his old dinner table, at the end of a meal, he

**looked across at his wife, and,
forgetting he was no longer the
incumbent, but a guest, remarked:**

**"I am afraid that we must put this
cook down as one of our failures."**

Another Church of Ireland Archbishop,
Whateley, had a dog of which he was
very fond. It was a smart animal and he
used to take it out on to St Stephen's
Green to throw things for it to catch, and
to teach it other tricks. Two old Dublin
ladies were watching him one day.

"Do you know who that fine gentleman
is? said one.

"No, but he's a fine, well set-up
gentleman, just the same."

"It's the Archbishop."

"Is that so indeed? God bless the

innocent creature. Isn't he easily amused, then."

"It's not our Archbishop, it's the Protestant one."

"Oh, the damn' oul' fool."

When gas was introduced, a Dubliner told her friend what an improvement it was over the coal range.

"I lit it two weeks ago," she said, "and it hasn't gone out yet."

Father O'Leary was a doughty champion of Catholic doctrine who nevertheless had many friends and admirers in the Church of Ireland. After they had been guests at the same dinner, the lawyer John Philpot Curran, not a great churchgoer, said to him:

"I wish you were St Peter."

"Why so, counsellor?" asked the priest.

"Because you might let me in, as master of the keys."

"It were better for you that I had the keys of the other place," said O' Leary, "for then I could let you out."

Bishop Woodward of the Church of Ireland had made an attack on the doctrine of Purgatory, upon which Father O'Leary observed:

"However clamorous a mitred divine might be about a Popish purgatory, he may perhaps go further, and fare worse."

Strolling home from the pub, along a boreen far out in the country, a man heard some cries coming from the hedge. Stooping down, he saw a leprechaun with his leg caught in a rabbit snare.

"Sure, I never saw that before," he muttered. "Maybe I had too much stout."

"Help me," said the leprechaun. "Get my leg out of this."

"Are you real then?" said the man.

"As real as you're drunk," it said. "But help me, and I'll give you three wishes."

Clumsily, the man managed to loosen the wire, and the leprechaun hopped free.

"Now," he said, "your wishes."

"I'd like a bottle of stout," said the man. Immediately, it was in his hand.

Mark Mechom

"And the next wish?"

The man drained the bottle.

"And for it never to be empty," he said. Immediately, it was full again. He gazed admiringly at it.

"And the third wish? Hurry up," said the leprechaun. "I'm late."

The man eyed him blearily.

"Just to be sure," he said, "I'll have another bottle that does the same."

Country Proverbs

When the cat is out, the dog is in.

Where there's a will, there's a won't.

When the wine is in, people drink it.

Man proposes, and woman refuses.

A stitch in time loses the race.

People who live in glass houses grow the best tomatoes.

Every cloud has a silver lining with a
hole in it.

**When the drop is inside, you don't
care if the sense is outside or not.**

The cracked pitcher is the one that
would otherwise have been a valuable
antique.

**He who gets a name for rising early
finds himself having to make the
porridge.**

A word to the wise earns a punch on the
nose.

**Sufficient unto the day is the apple
thereof.**

A fool and his money rush in where
angels fear to tread.

**Beware of a tight man
and a loose dog.**

A new bank robber was fully equipped.

"Remember, Seamus," the boss said, "you pull the tights over your head before we go in."

"The only trouble is," said Seamus, "I can't get them up further than me neck."

"**D**ennis," said his wife, "did you see that fine new hat and coat Mrs Culley was wearing in church today."

"No, I did not," said Dennis. "I'm afraid I was dozing off most of the time."

"Dennis!" exclaimed his wife. "A fat lot of good it does you to go to church."

A special fund had been organised by the new priest to pay for mending the leaky roof of the parish church. In charge was the treasurer, Mike Nolan. One evening the priest met Mr Nolan, and found him definitely the worse for wear.

"Mike," he said, "have you been at the pub?"

"No, Father," said Nolan. "I've been collectin' the sub-sub-whatd'youcallums for the church roof, an' everyone I called on insisted on me havin' a glass of whiskey with them."

"But surely not everyone in the parish is a whiskey drinker?"

"Oh, no, Father. I send my wee boy round to collect from them that isn't."

Dolan and Rafferty were fighting, and Dolan appeared to be getting the better of it.

"When you're beaten," said Dolan, "you should say you've had enough."

"If I have the strength to say I've had enough," gasped Rafferty, "then I'm not beaten yet."

When her husband returned home late with a black eye, a broken nose, and a split lip, Mrs Sullivan was shocked, but not surprised.

"What happened?" she asked.

"I got it fightin' with Pat Dugan," he said.

"Ye big stiff," said his wife. "Why, Pat

Dugan's just a little shrimp of a fellow.
How could you let a miserable
weakling like him do that to you?"
   "Hush, woman," said Sullivan.
"Speak no ill of the dead."

An Irish couple were being shown
round Texas by a guide who was anxious
to extol all the virtues of his native state.

   "Y'know," he said at one point, "Texas
is so big that your whole country of
Ireland could fit into one corner of it."

   "Aye," said the husband,
"and wouldn't that do
wonders for the place."

The only plumber in Dublin to charge reasonable rates died. Due to an administrative mix-up, he was sent to Hell. Eventually it was realised in Heaven that there was an honest plumber in the wrong place. St Peter got on the hot line to Satan.

"Have you got an honest plumber there?"

"Yes."

"Well, send him up. He's ours."

"You can't have him."

"What do you mean?"

"I'm getting him to put in air conditioning. It's going to be really cool down here soon."

"Send him up!" shouted St Peter. "Or we'll sue."

The voice at the other end laughed.

"You'll sue? And just where do you think you'll get hold of a lawyer?"

An American visitor had recently arrived at Shannon, and had hired a taxi driver to show him some of the sights. As they drove along the roads, he gave the driver some helpful information about his own country.

"Of course you're in the old world here," he said. "Everything takes a long time. I know. Back home, we can build a twenty-storey building in a fortnight. Here I guess it would take you two years."

The driver hunched his shoulders and said nothing. By and by they came in sight of the bulk of Bunratty Castle. Looking out of the window, the American whistled.

"What's that?" he asked.

"I don't know," said the taxi driver. "It wasn't there when I came by here yesterday."

The colonel of an Irish regiment called up a private soldier who had captured three enemy soldiers in battle. After commending his bravery he asked:

"And how did you manage to capture three men, single-handed?"

"Well, sir," replied the soldier, "I managed to surround them, so they just had to surrender."

A priest was talking encouragingly to a couple who were well-known for quarrelling all the time.

"Why, look at your cat and dog," he said. "They get on better than you two do."

"Try tying them together, and then see," said the man.

On their wedding night, Peggy and Dermot retired early to the honeymoon suite. Peggy was soon in bed, but she was surprised to see Dermot sitting down, fully dressed, in a chair.

"Aren't you coming to bed, dearest?" she asked.

"No fears," said Dermot. "My mother said this would be the best night of

my whole life and I'm not going to bed and missing any of it."

A well-known RTE sports commentator had to go to hospital for an operation. Despite his jolly screen personality, he turned out to be a nightmare patient. He shouted at the nurses, was rude to his fellow-patients, and questioned the doctors' knowledge, qualifications, and, when they weren't there, their parentage. He asked the lady with the library books if she had any porn. He found fault with absolutely everything.

One morning, a medical auxiliary whom he had not seen before came to take his temperature.

"Get on with it, woman," he said.

"No, no," she said. "I have to take it

from the other end. Doctor's orders."

After loud protest, he submitted to having his pyjama trousers pulled down, and the thermometer inserted in his anus.

"Stay like this for three minutes," she said. "I'll be right back."

Time passed.

He remained with his bottom in the air. After much more than three minutes he shouted, "What's going on?"

There was a sound of footsteps and the ward sister appeared. She looked at him and gasped.

"What's the matter?" he snarled. "Haven't you seen someone having his temperature taken before?"

"Not with a plastic daffodil," she said.

A troop of ramblers got lost and had to sleep in a cave on a hillside. In the morning their leader went out to prospect. Soon he was back.

"There is bad news and there is good news," he announced. "The bad news is that there's nothing to eat but sheep's droppings. The good news is that there's a huge supply of them."

"I always know when you're playing a spade," said one navvy card-player.

"How's that then?"

"It's that you spit on your hands before you take it up."

On a cold winter night Red Hanrahan went out to buy himself a half-bottle of whiskey. Stowing it away in his hip pocket, he set off home again. But on the icy road he slipped and fell. As he got to his feet, he felt something liquid trickling down his leg.

"Please God," he said, "let it be blood."

"When I die," said Tim O'Donovan to his best friend, "I want you to get a bottle of the finest Irish whiskey, and pour it over my grave. Will you do that?"

"Surely," said his friend. "You won't mind if I pass it through the kidneys first, will you?"

"**D**rink is a curse," announced the priest solemnly to his parishioners. "It makes you quarrel with your neighbours. It makes you get your gun out to shoot the landlord. And it makes you miss him."

"**A**nd how much of your neighbour's hay did you take?" asked the priest during a farmer's confession.

"Ah, well, your Reverence, I may as well confess to the whole stack while I'm about it. I'm going after the rest tonight."

An aeroplane passenger was looking rather nervous, so the stewardess came up to reassure him.

"Is it your first flight?" she asked.

"Indeed it is," he said.

"And are you feeling nervous?"

"Just a wee bit," he said. "I'm from Ahoghill, near Ballymena. No-one from the village has ever been in a plane before."

After an uneventful flight, the stewardess went up to him again.

"Were you comfy, sir?" she asked.

"I told you that already," he growled. "I'm from Ahoghill in County Antrim."